The New Novello Choral Edition

ROSSINI

Petite messe solennelle

for soprano, alto, tenor and bass soli,
SATB, harmonium and two pianos (ad.lib.) or orchestra

Vocal Score

NOVELLO PUBLISHING LIMITED

Order No: NOV 072436

It is requested that on all concert notices and programmes acknowledgement is made to 'The New Novello Choral Edition'.

The full score and orchestral material is available on hire from the Publisher.

A Chorus Score is available on sale (Order No: NOV 072452)

Novello is grateful to Christopher Hills for the corrections incorporated in the Second Reprint.

CONTENTS

PREFACE

Gioachino Rossini (1792-1868) referred to his *Petite messe solennelle* as 'the last mortal Sin of my Old Age'. Written in 1863 for the Countess Louise Pillet-Will and first performed on 14 March 1864 at the consecration of the Countess's private chapel, the Mass is one of Rossini's finest achievements and the outstanding work of his 'retirement'.

Originally written for 12 solo voices, 2 pianos and harmonium, Rossini subsequently arranged the accompaniment for orchestra (in 1867), while for publication the vocal parts were realigned into the present version for 4 solo voices and 8-part chorus.

This edition is based on Rossini's full score (published by Brandus, Paris, 1878). It can thus be used in performances of the orchestral version as well as with the harmonium and 2-piano accompaniment, though it should be noted that there is no distinct part for the second piano as it merely reinforced the first in certain passages.

Following the normal practice of the New Novello Choral Edition, single slurs in the vocal parts which indicate melismas of individual syllables have been replaced by hyphens or extension lines in the text. The remaining slurs are engraved as they appear in Rossini's manuscript.

1 KYRIE

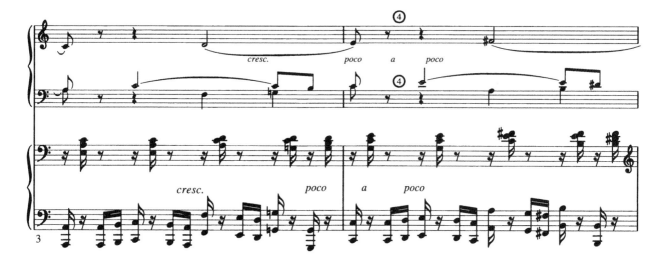

2

1

Soli and Chorus

ALTO
sotto voce

Ky - - ri - -

TENOR
sotto voce

Ky - - ri - - e, Ky - ri -

BASS
sotto voce

Ky - - ri - e, Ky - ri -

pp

cresc.

ppp

cresc. poco a poco

SOPRANO

4

5

23

25

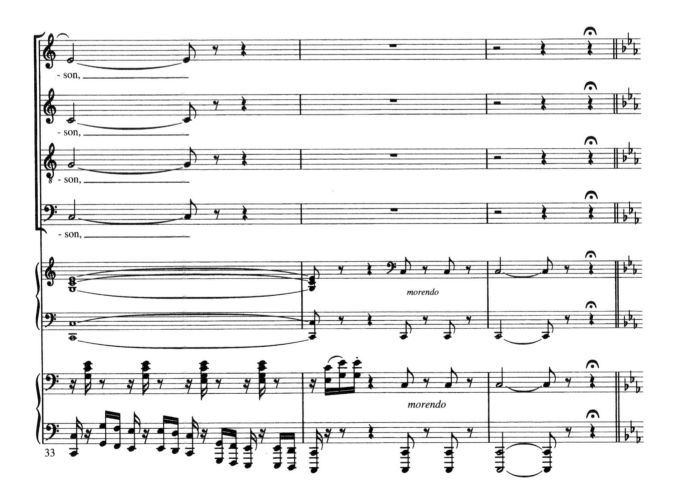

10

11

82

84

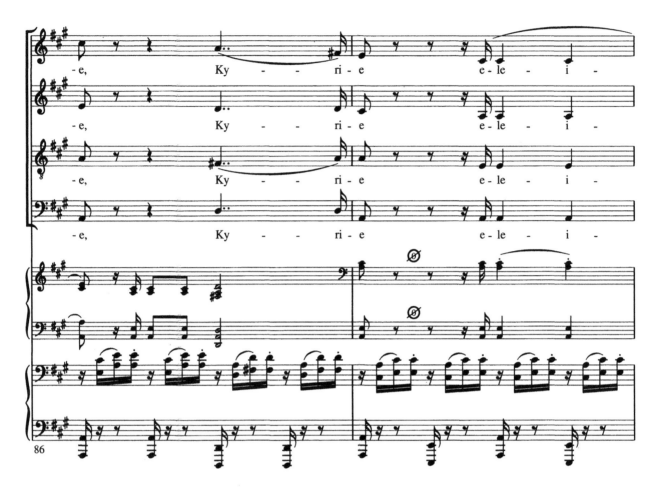

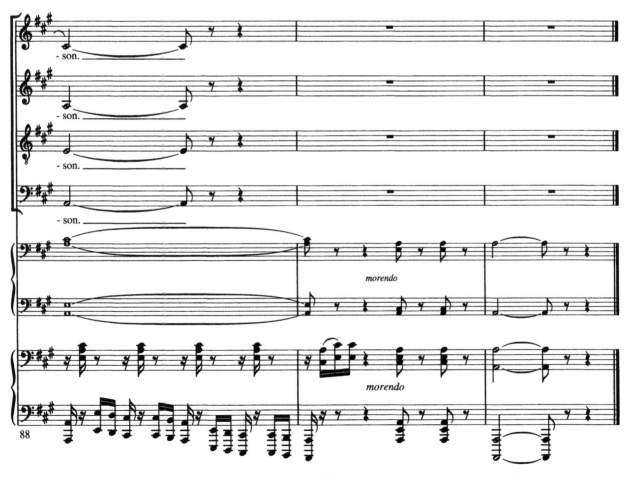

2 GLORIA

20

24

3 GRATIAS

glo - ri - am tu - - - am.

glo - ri - am tu - - - am.

glo - ri - am tu - - - am.

smorz.

pppp

56

ff

pp

61

9
ppp

Gra - ti - as a - gi - mus ti - - bi

ppp

Gra - ti - as a - gi - mus, a - gi - mus ti - bi

ppp

Gra - ti - as a - gi - mus, a - gi - mus ti - bi____

9

ppp

66

4 DOMINE DEUS

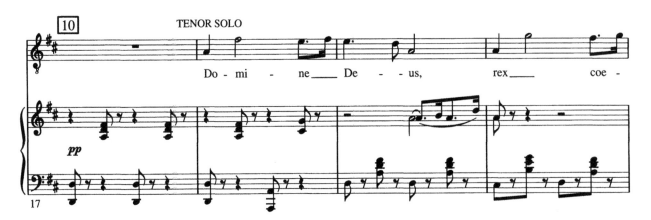

Do - mi - ne___ De - us, rex___ coe -

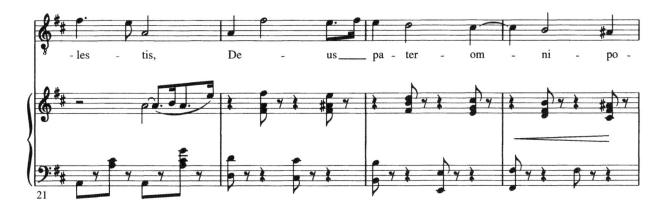

34

Chris - te, Do - mi - ne___ De - us,___ rex___ coe -

37

- les - tis, De - us___ pa - ter om - ni - po -

41

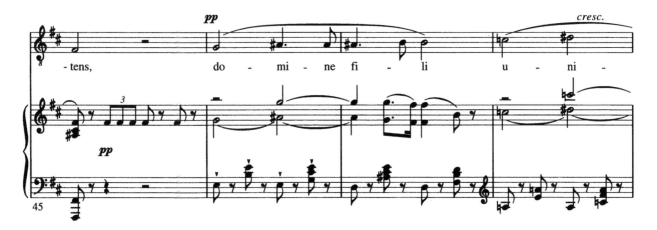

- tens, do - mi - ne fi - li u - ni -

45

- ge - ni - te, u - ni - ge - ni - te, Je - su Chris -

49

fi - li - us pa - - tris,

73

do - - mi - ne De - us, a - gnus De - i,

77

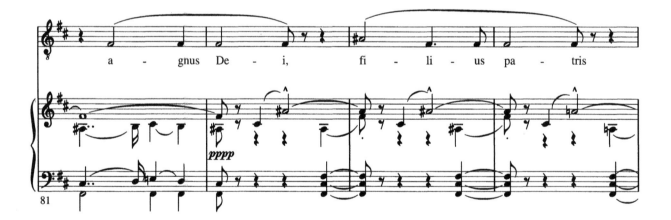

a - gnus De - i, fi - li - us pa - tris

81

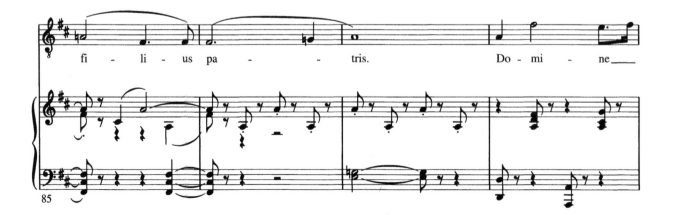

fi - li - us pa - - tris. Do - mi - ne___

85

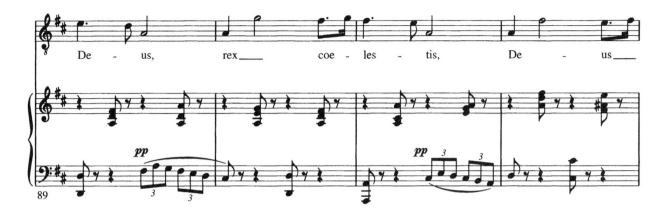

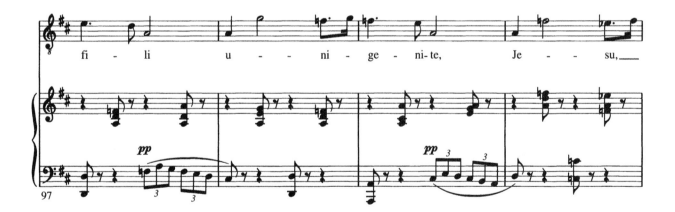

De - us, rex___ coe - les - tis, De - us___

pa - ter om - ni - po - tens,___ do - mi - ne___

fi - li u - ni - ge - ni - te, Je - su,___

Je - su___ Chris - te,___ Je - su

Chris - te, Je - su Chris - te, Do - mi - ne__

105

De - us,__ rex__ coe - les - tis, De - us__

109

pa - ter om - ni - po - tens, do - mi - ne

113

fi - li u - ni - ge - ni - te, u - ni -

117

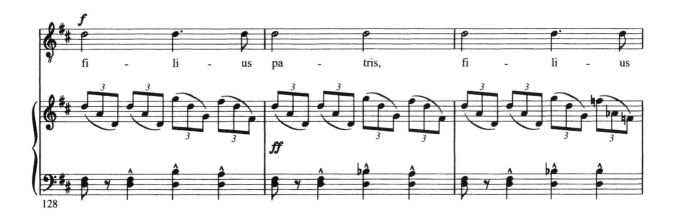

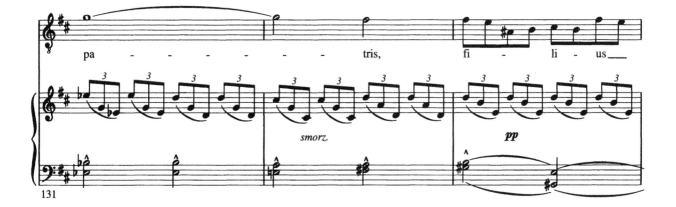

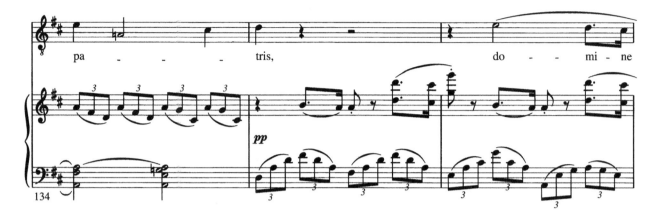

pa - - - tris, do - mi - ne

134

De - us, a - gnus___ De - i,

cresc. *f*

137

f
fi - li - us pa - tris, fi - li - us

ff

140

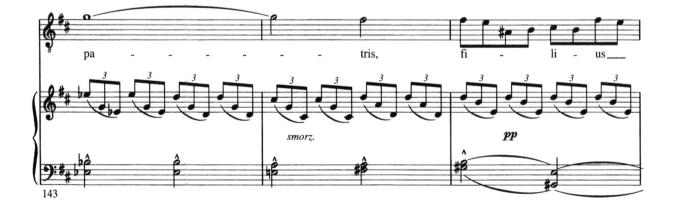

pa - - - - - tris, fi - li - us___

smorz. *pp*

143

pa - - - tris, fi - li - us pa - - tris, fi - li - us

pa - - tris.

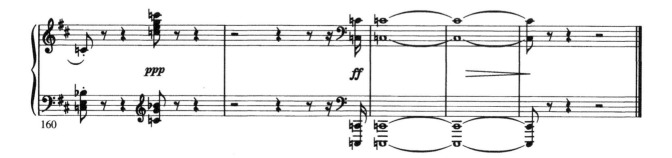

5 QUI TOLLIS

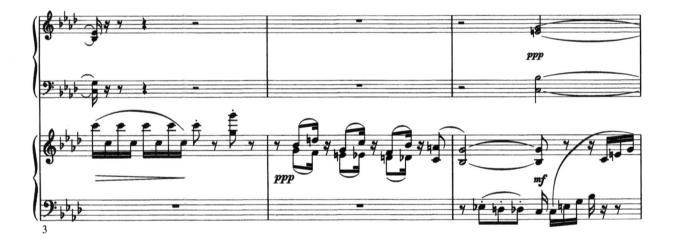

SOPRANO SOLO

Qui

ALTO SOLO

Qui

tol - - lis   pec- ca - - ta,   pec-

tol - - lis   pec- ca - - ta,   pec-

-ca - - ta   mun - - di

-ca - - ta   mun - - di

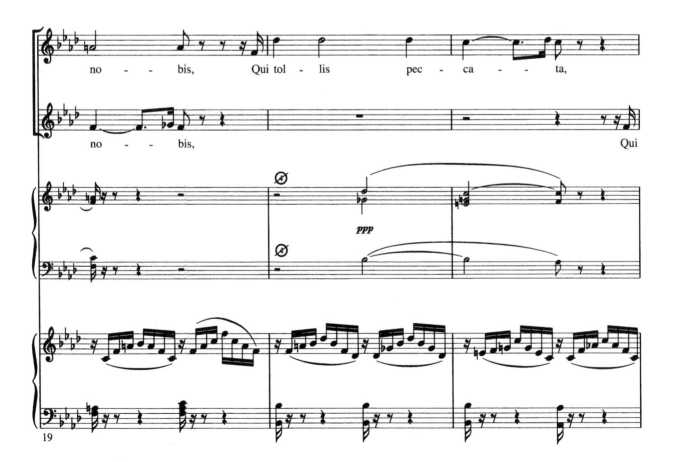

46

28

31

48

-ca - ta___ mun - di su - sci - - pe

40

de - pre - ca - ti - o - nem nos - - tram,___

Qui

43

tol - - lis pec - ca - - ta, pec - ca - - ta_____

mun - - di su - sci - - pe de - pre - ca - ti -

52

mi - se - re - - re no - - bis, mi - se - re - re

mi - se - re - re no - - bis, mi - se - re - - re

62

no - - bis. Qui se - des ad dex - - te - ram,

no - - bis. Qui

65

54

74

77

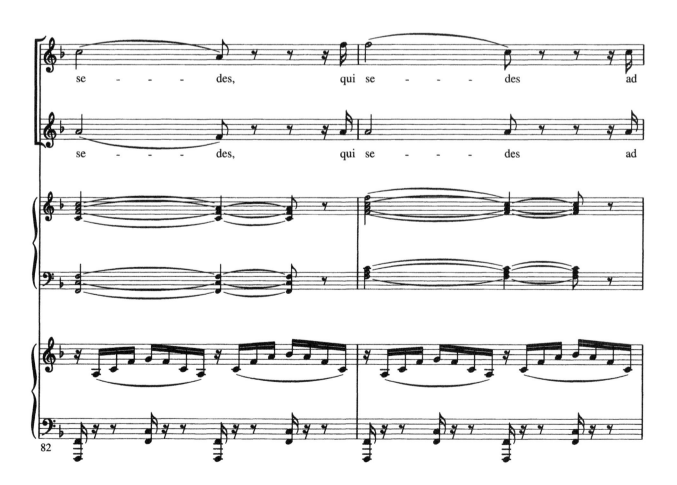

dex - - te - ram___ pa - - tris, qui

dex - - te - ram___ pa - - tris, qui

84

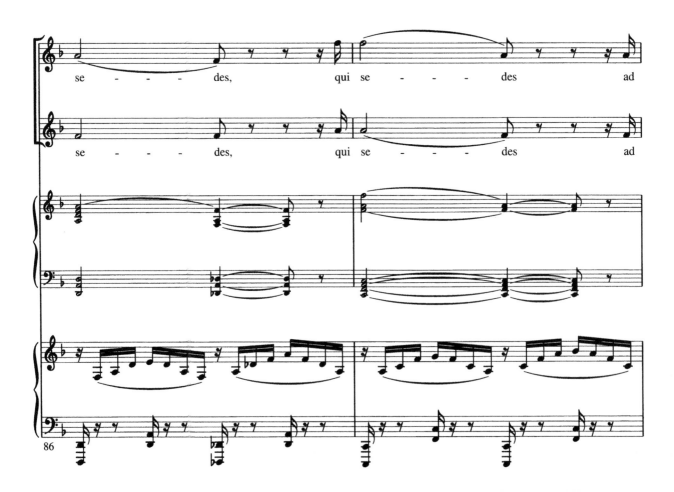

se - - - des, qui se - - des ad

se - - - des, qui se - - des ad

86

dex - te - ram pa - - tris, mi - se - re - re,

dex - te - ram pa - - tris, mi - se -

88

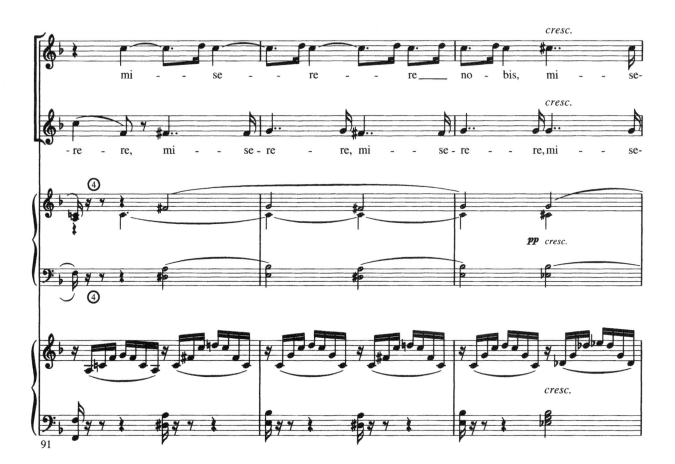

cresc.

mi - se - re - re ___ no - bis, mi - se-

cresc.

- re - re, mi - se - re - re, mi - se - re - re, mi - se-

91

-re - - re,_____ no - - bis, mi - se-

-re - - re,_____ no - - bis, mi - se-

94

- re - re,_____ no - - bis, mi - se-

- re - re,_____ no - - bis,

96

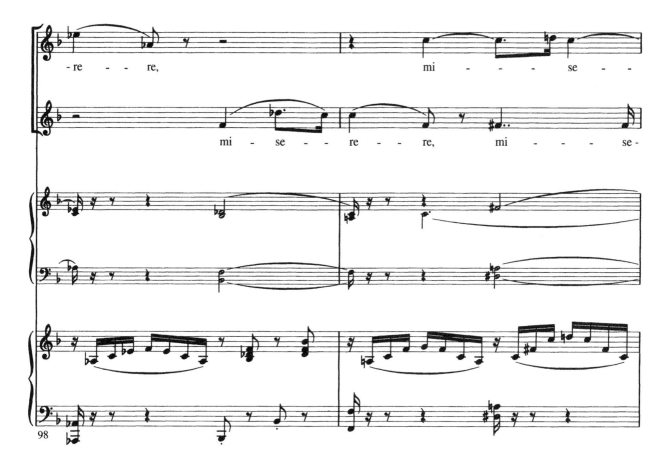

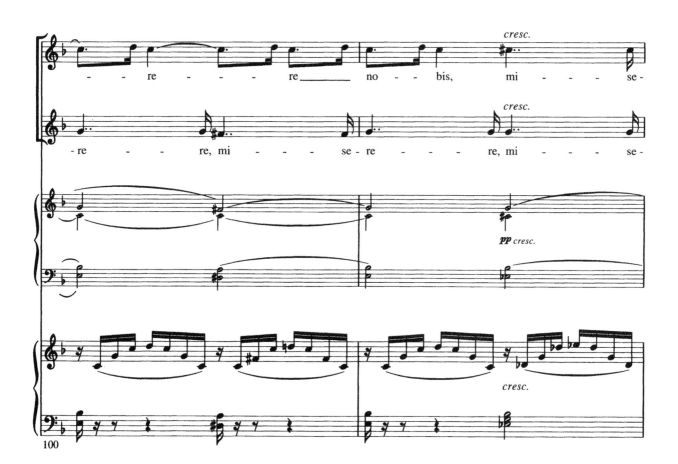

60

102

104

106

108

110

6 QUONIAM

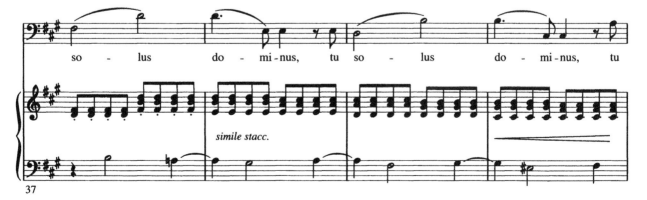

64

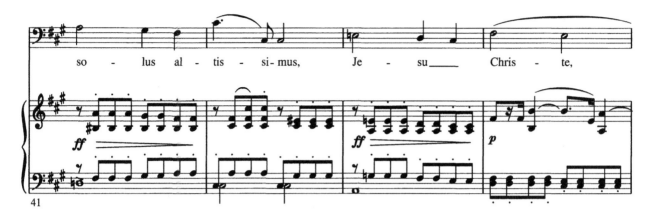

so - lus al - tis - si - mus, Je - su Chris - te,

41

Je - su, Je - su Chris- te, tu

45

so - lus, tu so - lus al - tis - si - mus, al -

49

-tis - si - mus, Je - su Chris - te, tu so - lus al -

53

-tis - si - mus, Je - su,__ Je - su__ Chris - - - -

- te,

tu so - lus

sanc - tus, tu so - lus do - mi - nus tu so - lus al -

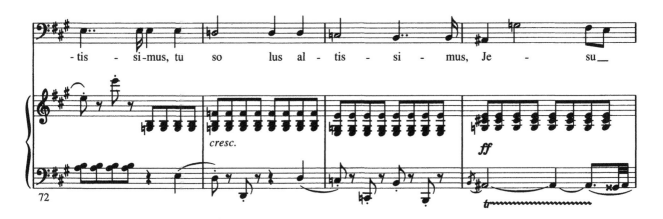

-tis - si-mus, tu so lus al - tis - si - mus, Je - su____

72

Chris-te.   Quo - ni-am tu

76

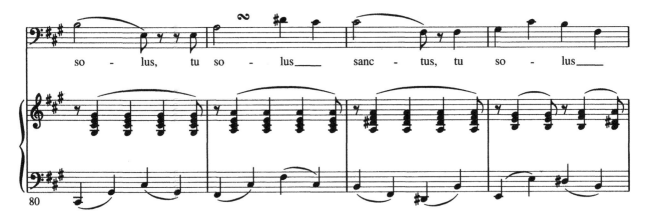

so - lus, tu so - lus____ sanc - tus, tu so - lus____

80

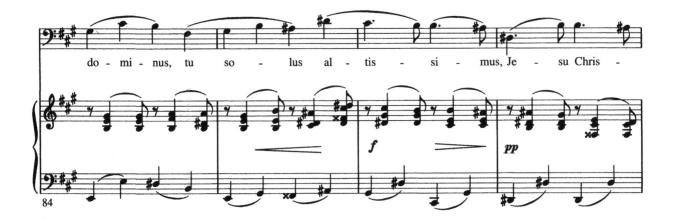

do - mi - nus, tu so - lus al - tis - si - mus, Je - su Chris -

84

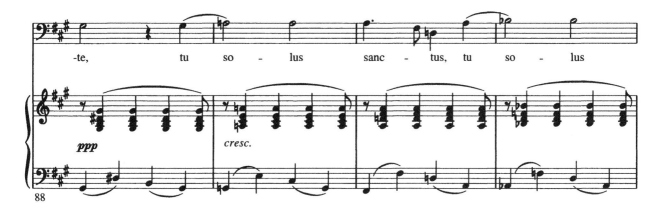

68

al - tis - si - mus, Je - su

Chris - - - - te, tu

so - - lus, tu so - - lus al - tis - si - mus, al -

- tis - si - mus, Je - - su Chris - - te,_____ tu

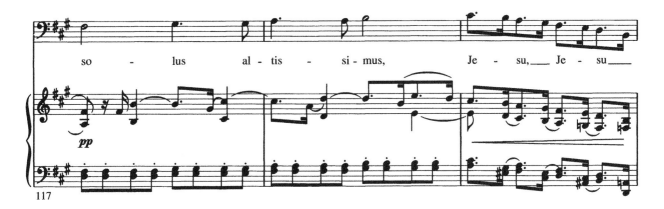

so - lus al - tis - si - mus, Je - su,___ Je - su___

Chris - - - te,

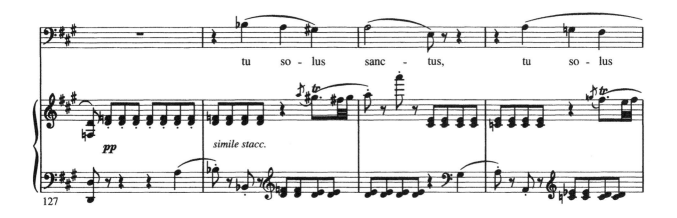

tu so - lus sanc - tus, tu so - lus

70

do - mi - nus,   tu   so - lus al - tis - - si - mus, tu   so - lus al -

cresc.

131

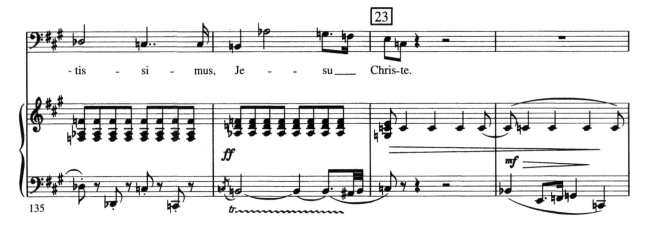

23

- tis - - si - - mus,   Je - - su____ Chris - te.

ff

mf

135

tr

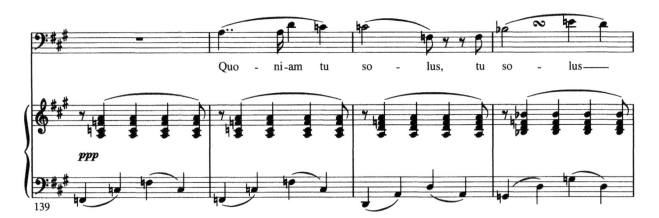

Quo - ni - am tu   so - - lus,   tu   so - lus——

ppp

139

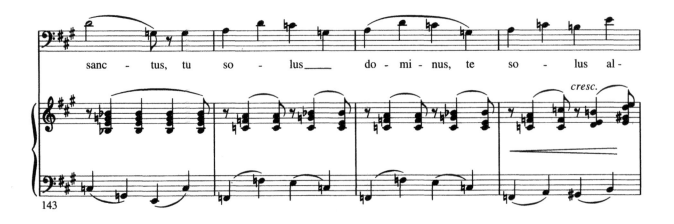

sanc - tus, tu   so - lus____ do - mi - nus, te   so - lus al -

cresc.

143

-tis - si - mus, Je - su Chris - te, tu so - lus

sanc - tus, tu so - lus do - mi - nus, tu so - lus al -

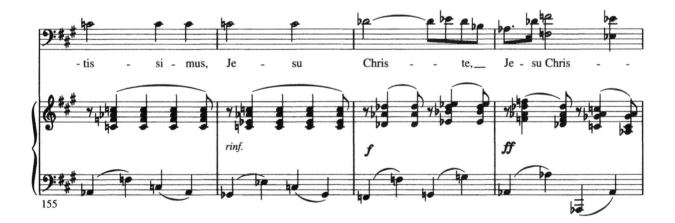

-tis - si - mus, Je - su Chris - te,__ Je - su Chris -

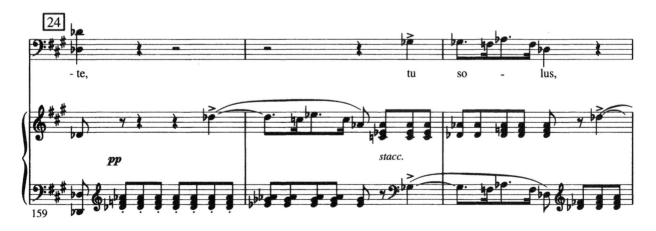

-te, tu so - lus,

72

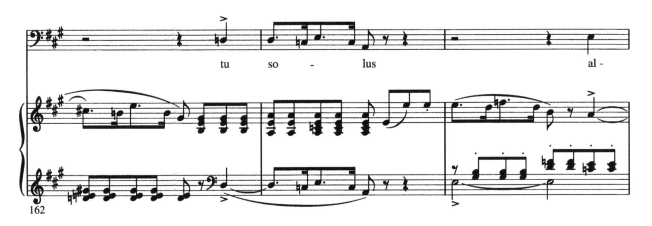

162

165

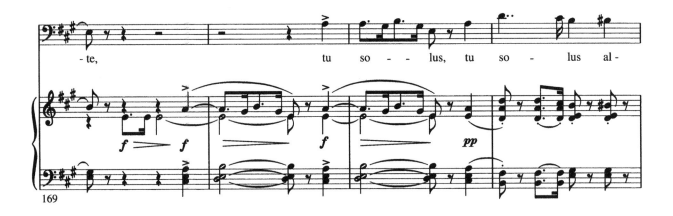

169

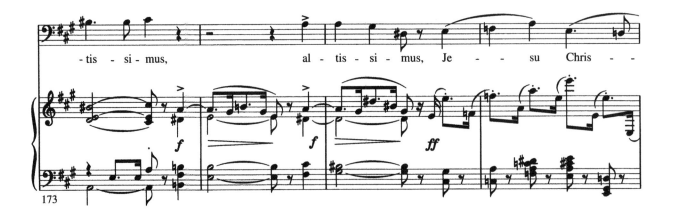

173

73

74

Subito
Cum Sancto Spiritu

7 CUM SANCTO SPIRITU

- men, A - - - - men, A - - -

spi - ri - tu in glo - ri - a De - i pa - tris. A - - men,____

34

- - - - - - - men, A - - - - -

____ A - - - - men, A - -

TENOR

Cum sanc - to spi - ri - tu in

38

82

66

70

84

82

86

- - - men,
- - - men, A - - men, A - - - -
- men._____ Cum sanc - to spi - ri - tu in glo - ri - a De - i

90

A - - - - - - - - -
- men, A - - - men, A - - - -
pa - tris. A - - men,_____ A - - - -

94

86

spi - ri-tu in glo-ri-a De - i pa - tris. A - - - - men,____

A - - - - - - - men, A - -

A - - - - - - - - - - - men, A - -

- - men, A - - - - - - - - - - -

— A - - - - - - - - men, A - -

- - - - - - - - - - - men, A - - -

- - - - - - - - men, A - -

- - - - - - - - - men, A - men,_____ A - -

138

142

92

146

150

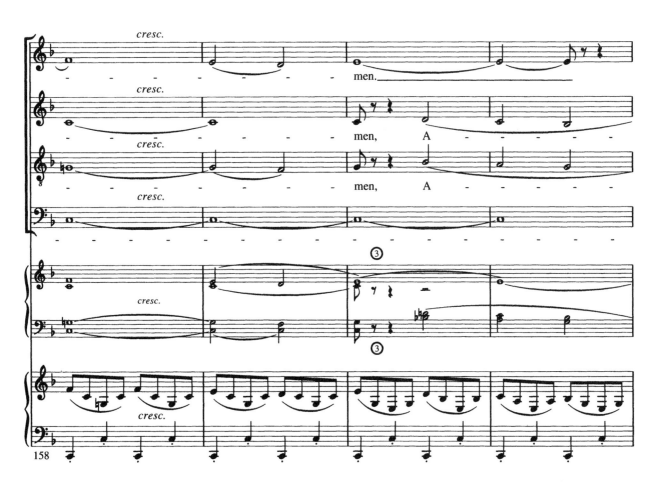

Cum sanc - to spi - ri - tu in glo - ri - a De - i pa - tris. A - -

- men, A - - - - men.

- men, A - - - - - - - - men, A - -

- men,

162 stacc.

- men, A - - - men, A - - - - - - - -

Cum sanc - to spi - ri - tu in glo - ri - a De - i pa - tris. A - -

- men, A - - - - - men.

A - - - - - - - - men, A - -

166

men, A — — — — — — — men, A — —

men, A — — — — — — — — — — men,

Cum sanc-to spi-ri-tu in glo-ri-a De-i pa-tris. A —

men, A — — — — — men.

170

men, A — — — — — — — — — —

A — — — — — — — men, A —

men, A

Cum sanc-to spi-ri-tu in glo-ri-a De-i pa-tris. A —

174

96

178

182

186

190

194

198

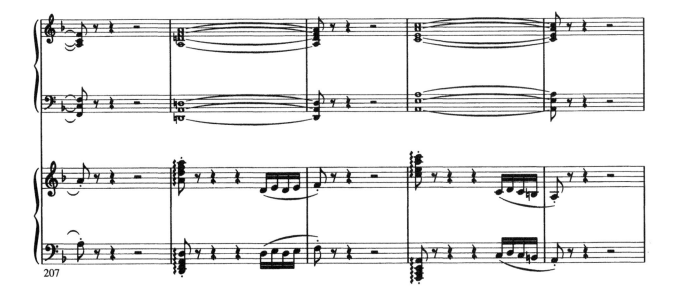

100

Glo - ri - a in ex - cel - sis,

Glo - ri - a in ex - cel - sis,

Glo - ri - a in ex - cel - sis,

Glo - ri - a in ex - cel - sis,

212

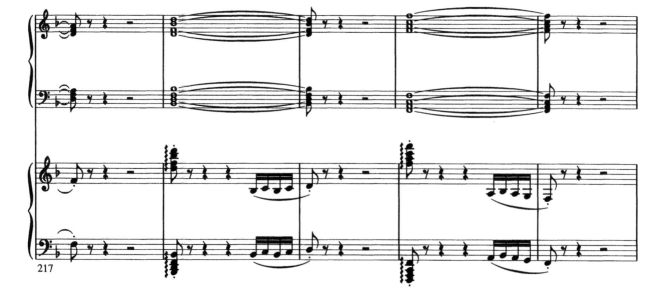

217

in ex - cel - sis De - o, A - men,

in ex - cel - sis De - o, A -

in ex - cel - sis De - o, A -

in ex - cel - sis De - o, A -

Animando un poco

Animando un poco

Animando un poco

222

— A - men, A - men,

- men, A - men, A -

- men, A - men, A -

- men, A - men, A -

227   sim.

102

231

235

106

8 CREDO

110

112

49

53

114

64

68

72

76

80

83

118

92

95

98

101

fac - - tus est._____

fac - - tus est._____

127

130

133

124

9 CRUCIFIXUS

5

no - bis sub Pon - ti - o Pi - la - to, sub Pon - ti - o Pi-

-la - to, pas - sus,____ pas - sus et se - pul - tus

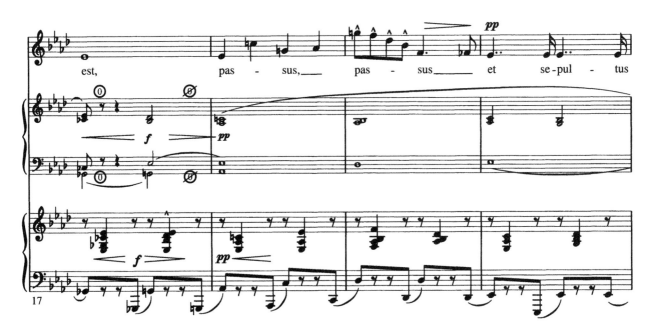

est, pas - sus,____ pas - sus____ et se - pul - tus

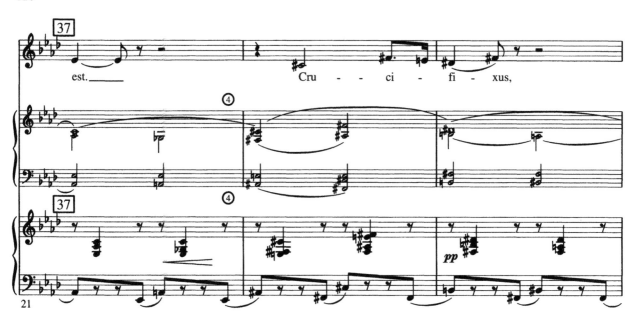

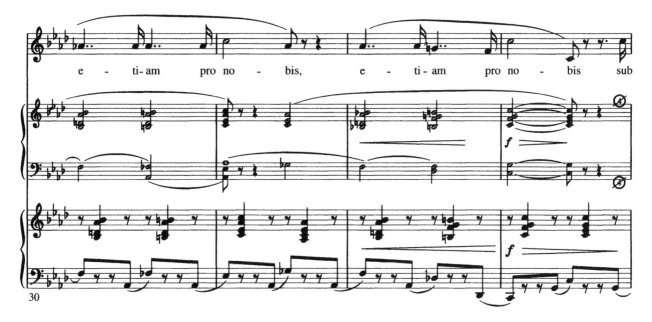

e - ti- am pro no - bis, e - ti- am pro no - bis sub

30

Pon - ti-o Pi - la - to, sub Pon - ti-o Pi - la - to,

34

pas - sus,___ pas - sus et sep-ul - tus est,_____

38

128

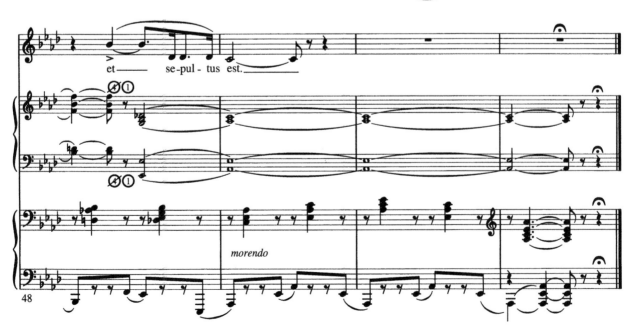

10 ET RESURREXIT

130

132

x

coe - lum,
SOLO
coe - lum, a - scen - dit in
coe - lum,
SOLO
coe - lum, et a - scen - dit, a - scen - dit in
33
SOLO
se - det ad dex - te-ram, se - det ad
coe - lum, se - det ad dex - te-ram, se - det ad
SOLO
se - det ad
coe - lum, se - det ad dex - te-ram, se - det ad
37

glo - ri - a ju - di -
glo - ri - a ju - di -
glo - ri - a ju - di -
glo - ri - a ju - di - ca - re

47

- ca - re_____ vi - vos et___ mor - tu -
- ca - re vi - vos et mor - tu -
- ca - re vi - vos et___ mor - tu -
vi - vos, vi - vos et mor - tu -

50

65

68

et glo - ri - fi - ca - tur,

et glo - ri - fi - ca - tur,

pp

ff

ff

79

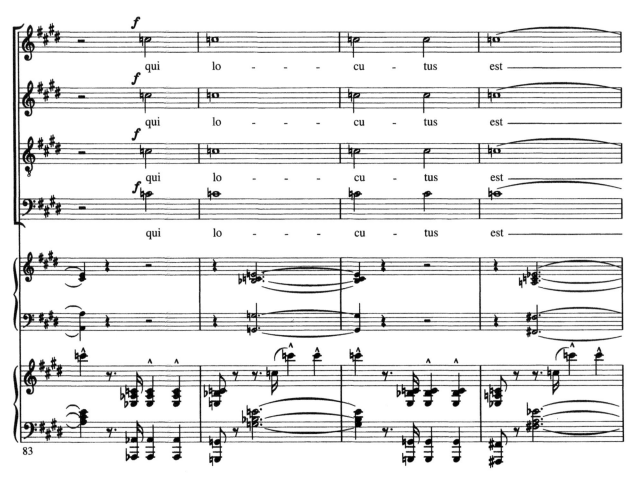

qui lo - - cu - tus est

qui lo - - cu - tus est

qui lo - - cu - tus est

qui lo - - cu - tus est

83

96

100

146

22

130

133

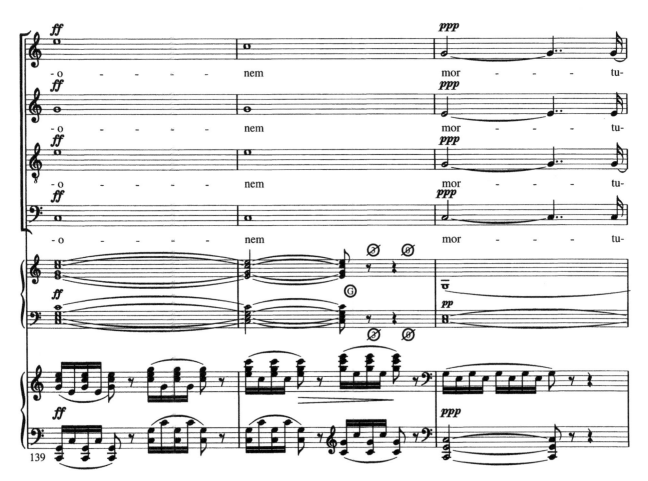

148

151

42 **Allegro** ($\circ$ = **108**)

et vi - tam ven - tu - ri sae - cu - li. A - men, A -

A - - - - - - - - - - -

42 **Allegro** ($\circ$ = **108**)

sim.

155

191

196

156

211

216

231

236

241

246

251

256

291

295

299

303

307

311

325

329

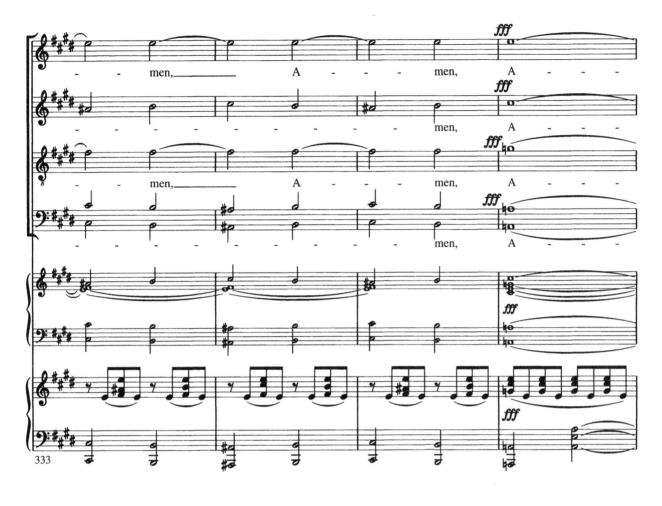

341

345

358

364

11 PRELUDIO RELIGIOSO

(Offertory)

HARMONIUM or PIANO

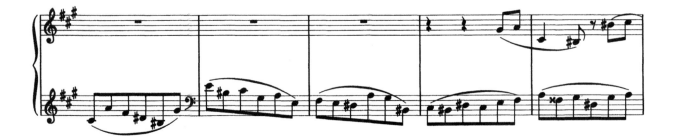

178

102

107

112

117

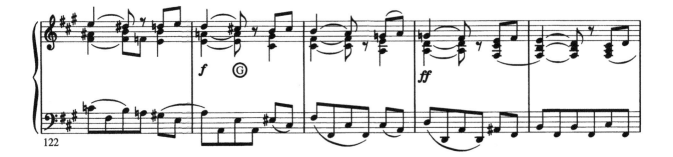

122

Ritornello

12 SANCTUS

13 O SALUTARIS

SOPRANO SOLO

O sa - lu - ta - ris hos - ti - a quae coe - li pan -

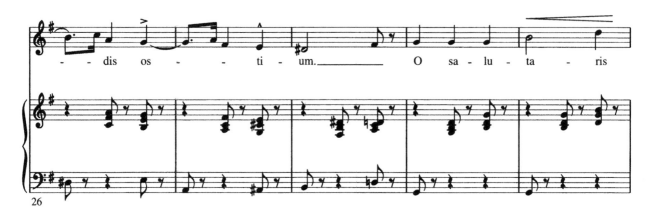

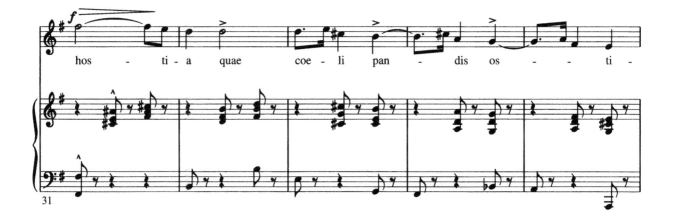

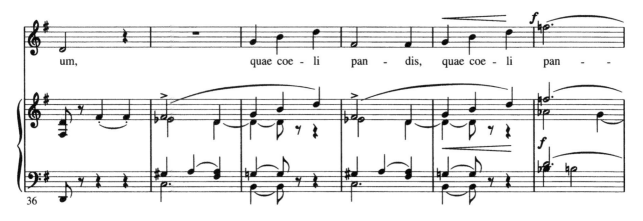

ritornando al tempro primo

- xi - - li - um.____

48

O sa - lu - ta - ris hos - ti -

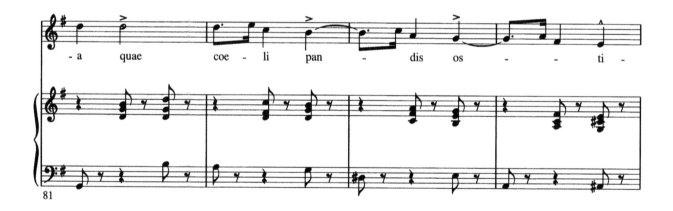

- a quae coe - li pan - dis os - ti -

- um._____ O sa - lu - ta - ris hos - ti -

189

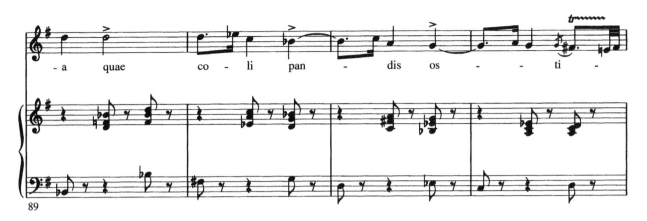

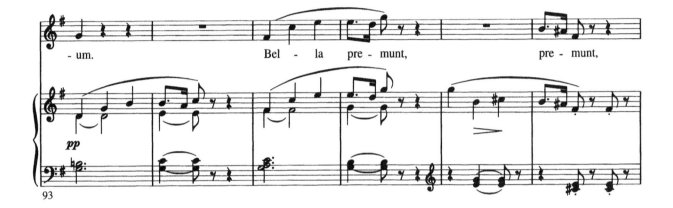

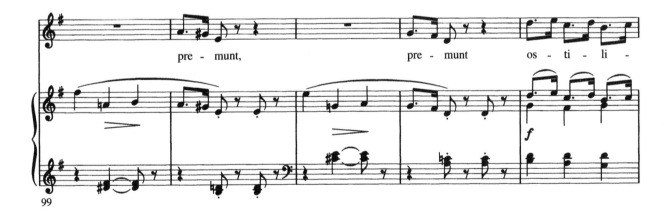

da ro - bur fer au - xi - li - um, da___ ro - bur___

fer au - xi - li - um, da___ ro - bur fer_____ au -

-xi - li - um.   Bel - la pre - munt hos-

-ti - li - a,   bel - la pre - munt hos - ti - li - a,

191

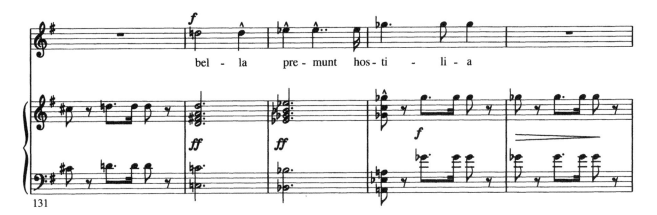

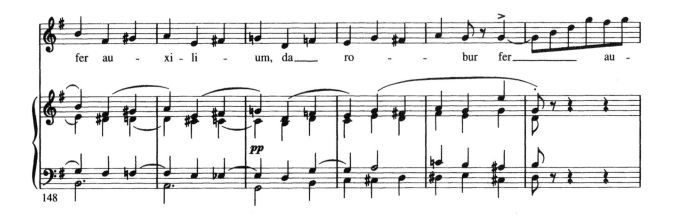

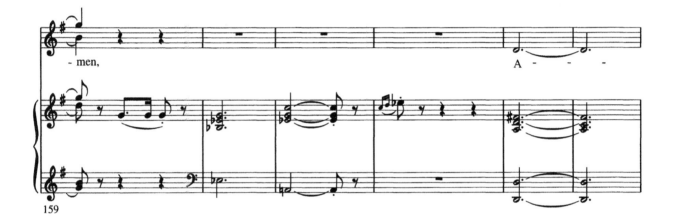

14 AGNUS DEI

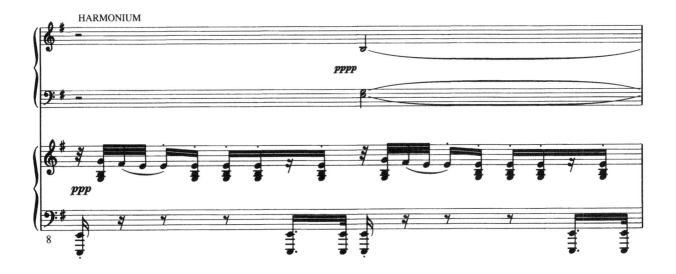

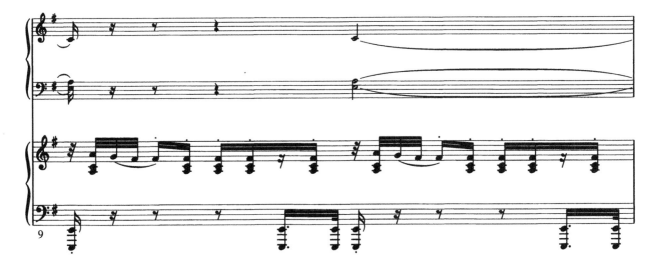

198

no - - - bis, qui tol - lis pec -

- - ca - - ta, pec - ca - ta

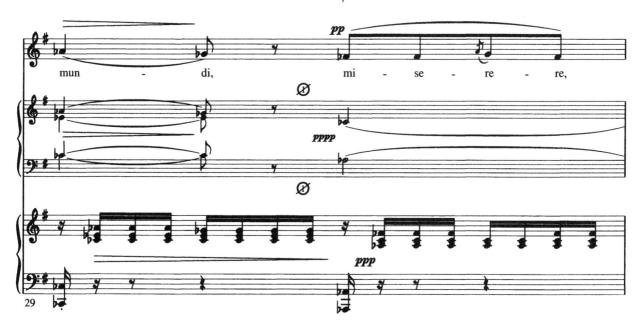

mun - - di, mi - se - re - re,

200

mun - di, do - na no - bis pa -

- cem,_____ do - na no - bis, pa -

- cem,_____ do - na no - bis, do - na_

no - bis, do - na, do - na_____ no - bis_ pa -

- cem.

SOPRANO *sotto voce*

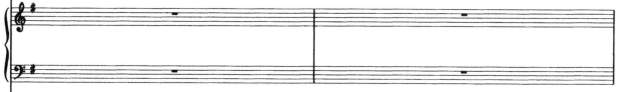

Do - na no - bis_ pa - cem, do - na no - bis_ pa - - -

ALTO *sotto voce*

Do - na no - bis pa - cem, do - na no - bis pa - - -

TENOR *sotto voce*

Do - na no - bis_ pa - cem, do - na no - bis_ pa - - -

BASS *sotto voce*

Do - na no - bis pa - cem, do - na no - bis pa - - -

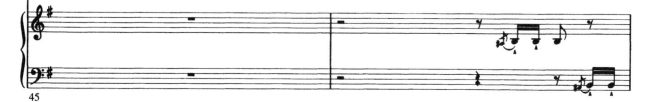

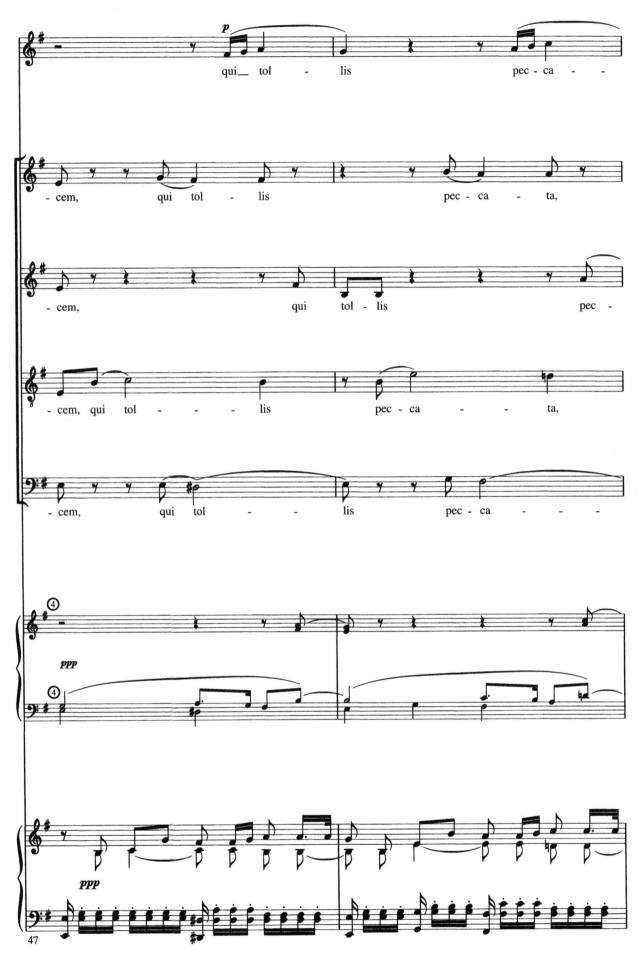

47

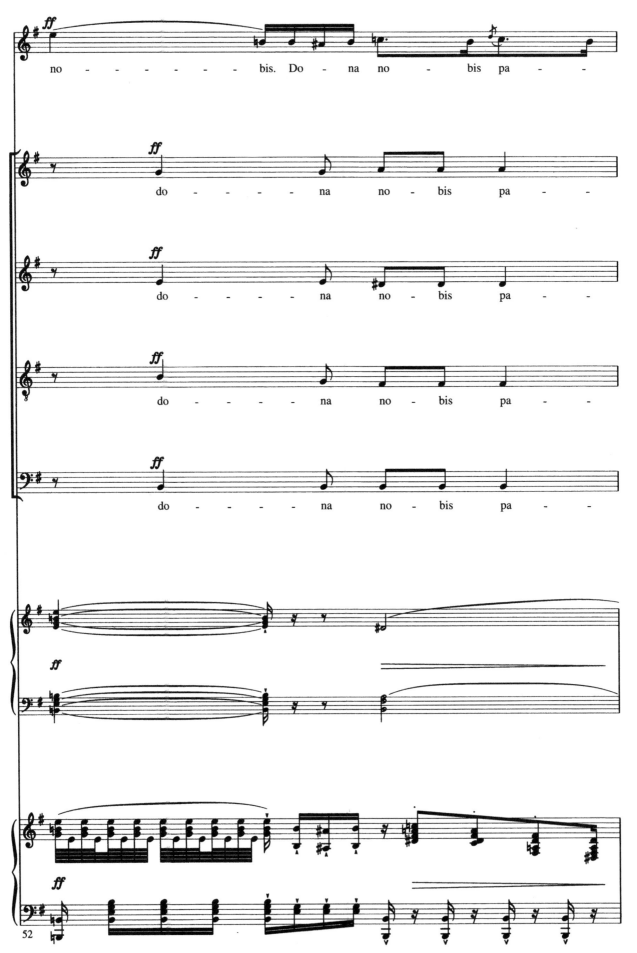

208

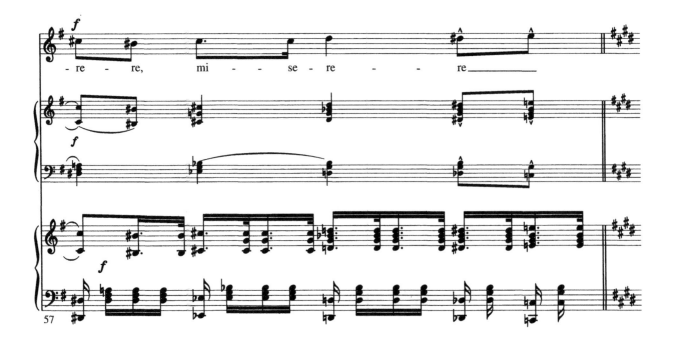

no - - - - bis__ pa -

do - na no - bis pa - - - - - - -

do - na no - bis pa - - - - - - -

do - na no - bis pa - - - - - - -

do - na no - bis pa - - - - - -

59

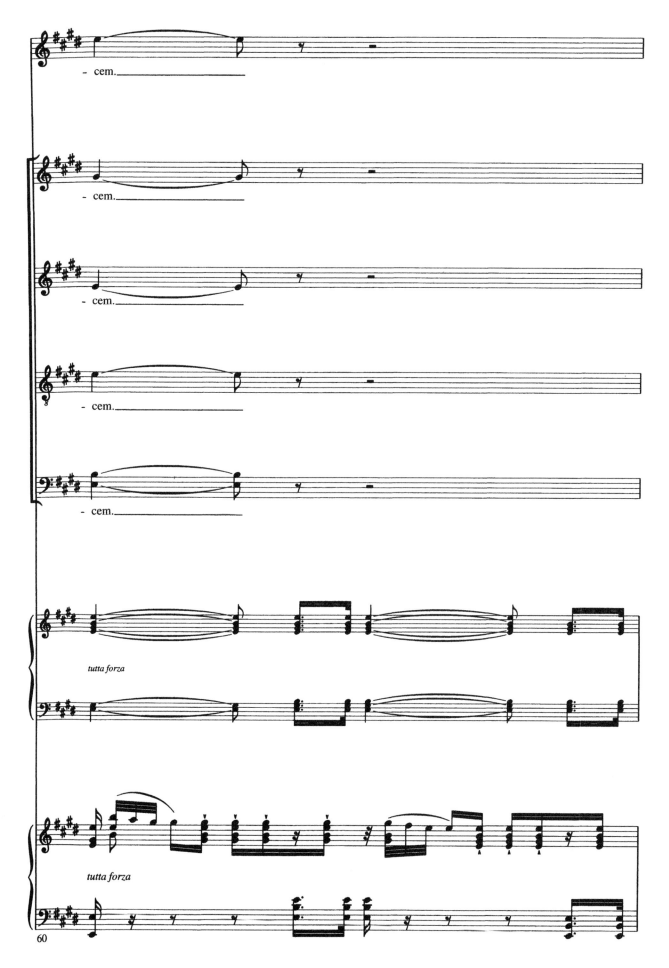

- cem.

- cem.

- cem.

- cem.

- cem.

tutta forza

tutta forza

60

212

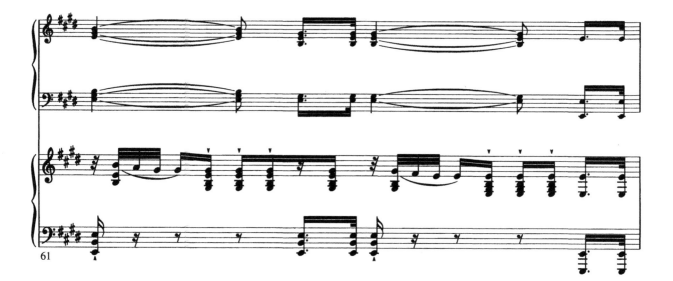

61

62

66

Printed in Great Britain by Caligraving Ltd., Thetford, Norfolk